PORTSMOUTH

TO

SOUTHAMPTON

Vic Mitchell and Keith Smith

Design – Deborah Goodridge

First published – June 1986

ISBN 0 906520 31 2

© *Middleton Press, 1986.*

Published by Middleton Press
Easebourne Lane
Midhurst, West Sussex.
GU29 9AZ
☎ *073 081 3169*

Phototypeset by CitySet · Bosham 573270

Printed & bound by Biddles Ltd,
Guildford and Kings Lynn.

CONTENTS

ACKNOWLEDGEMENTS

We would like to express our appreciation of the assistance received from those mentioned in the photograph credits and also from Mrs E. Fisk, V. Harris, N. Langridge, R. Randell and N. Stanyon.
As ever our gratitude is immeasurable for our patient wives.

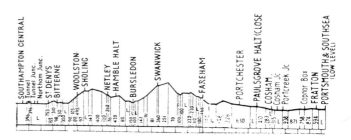

GEOGRAPHICAL SETTING

After traversing the relatively level land of Portsea Island, the line rises slightly onto the lower slopes of Portsdown Hill, whilst running parallel to the northern shore of Portsmouth Harbour. West of Fareham, the small River Meon is crossed before the route rises onto the fertile area which stretches to the larger River Hamble at Bursledon. A further circuitous climb is necessary to cross the high land between the Hamble and Itchen Valleys. The route runs north close to the River Itchen, crosses it about two miles from its mouth and then runs south on the opposite shore to Southampton. The geographical features which have made this city an ideal port are its location on protected inland deep water and its unusual four high tides per day, due to its relationship to the Isle of Wight.

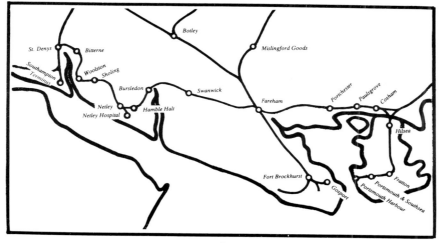

HISTORICAL BACKGROUND

Services between London and Southampton commenced on 11th May 1840, although trains had run between Winchester and Northam Road since 10th June 1839. A branch from Eastleigh (then known as Bishopstoke) was opened to Gosport on 21st November 1841 by the London & Southampton Railway, whose title was soon changed to the London & South Western Railway. The London, Brighton & South Coast Railway extended its line from Chichester to Portsmouth in 1847 and, in the following year, formed a joint committee with the LSWR to operate the railway on Portsea Island. This allowed the latter company's trains to operate direct to Portsmouth from Fareham, via Cosham. The line was extended to the Harbour station on 2nd October 1876.

In 1863, a large military hospital was opened at Netley and sick and injured servicemen returning from Overseas were landed at its pier. To improve transport to and from Netley a single line railway was opened from St. Denys (then Portswood) on 5th March 1866. (It was extended to the Hospital on 18th April 1900). The need to link Portsmouth and Southampton was low priority and so it was not until 2nd September 1889 that a single line between Netley and Fareham was eventually opened.

1902 saw the quadrupling of the tracks between St. Denys and Northam and the line between St. Denys and Fareham was doubled in 1909-11.

route took place 30 years apart – London to Portsmouth in 1937 and London to Southampton in 1967.

Dieselisation of local services on the route took place between 1957 and 1959, with the introduction of DEMUs. Western Region DMUs were used on cross country trains from 1965 to 1968, after which locomotive hauled services were restored, although by then, entirely diesel powered.

NO SURRENDER.

Brother Townsmen,

Will you tamely submit to be crushed by that great Juggernaut, the South Western Railway Company?

Will you for ever betray your own Interests by supine Indolence, now when Victory is almost within your reach?—Listen not to the coaxing of the friends of the all-monopolizing Dictators; believe not their idle reports; attend, hear all parties, judge for yourselves.

Bestir yourselves, and like a Lion roused from his slumbers, show by an early attendance THIS EVENING, in the Society Hall, that you prize the Interests of your fellow Townsmen, your Families, and the lasting prosperity of the Neighbourhood, by supporting

A Cheap and Independent Line of Railway.

MONDAY, *Jan. 19th,* 1846.

A WELL WISHER.

PASSENGER SERVICES

For most of the years that Netley was the terminus of a branch line, seven trains on weekdays only were provided. After the extension to Fareham, there were six through trains and three short workings, still weekdays only. By 1910, 16 through services operated with two local journeys and two Sunday trains.

Frequency had increased and some destinations were more remote by the end of the 1930s. For example, in 1938 22 trains passed each way on weekdays, four of them originating at Brighton, and 10 ran on Sundays. The SR expanded the western destinations to include Bournemouth, Plymouth, Bristol and Cardiff but services were reduced by about a third during WWII.

September 1957 saw the introduction of a regular interval service on the route, with a stopping and semi-fast train each hour, in addition to the long distance trains. Subsequent cut-backs have resulted in a basic service of an hourly slow train (sometimes extended to Salisbury) and an hourly fast train to Bristol, or beyond. However, in 1983 a through service to Penzance (from Brighton) on Fridays was added, although it terminated at Plymouth during the winter.

Additional services have operated between Fareham and Portsmouth in connection with the Meon Valley and Eastleigh routes. The former are summarised in our *Branch Lines to Alton* and the latter will be mentioned in a later album.

Accelerated and Improved Through Service
BETWEEN
BRIGHTON WORTHING CHICHESTER
AND
SOUTHAMPTON BOURNEMOUTH
EXETER PLYMOUTH ILFRACOMBE Etc.

On Week Days.

	a.m.	a.m.	p.m.			a.m.	a.m.	a.m.
Hastings ... dep	8 15	10 38	12 50	Plymouth (North Road.) dep		9 38	10 40	
St. Leonards (W. Sq.) ,,	8 18	10 41	12 53	Padstow ..			10 5	
St. Leonards (W. M.) ,,	8 22	10 45	12 58	Wadebridge ..			10 17	
Bexhill Central ,,	8 30	10 53	1 6	Bude ..		7 20	11 5	
Eastbourne ,,	8 40	11 0	1 5	Ilfracombe ..		8 50	10A10	
Seaford .. ,,	8 47	10 23	1 18	Torrington ..		9 10	10 30	
Newhaven Harbour ,,	8 53	10 29	1 24	Bideford ..		9 19	10 39	
Lewes .. ,,	9 14	11 21	1 45	Barnstaple Junction ..		9 47	11 8 9	
		non		Exeter (St. David's) ..		11 34	1 2	
Brighton .. .. .. dep	9 40	12 0	2 30	Exeter (Queen Street) ..		11 45	1 13	
		p.m.		Sidmouth ..		10 55		
Hove .. ,,	9 44	12 5	2 34	Lyme Regis .. ,,		11 35		
Worthing .. ,,	9 56	12 21	2 48				p.m.	
Arundel .. ,,		11 58	2 46	Salisbury .. ,,		1 48	3 5	
Littlehampton ,,	9 25	12 20	2 55	Fareham .. ,,		3 17	4 8	
Bognor .. ,,	9 37	12 25	2035					
Chichester .. ,,	10 21	12 56	3 19	Bournemouth { West .. dep	10 36	1 40		
Fareham .. arr		1 28	4 30	{ Central. ,,	10 48	1 52		
				Boscombe ..	10 53	1 57		
Portsmouth and				Pokesdown ..	10 56	2 0		
Southsea .. .. dep			4 10	Christchurch ..	11 2	2 6		
Fareham .. arr		1 28	4 30	New Milton ..		2 17		
Netley .. ,,		2 21		Brockenhurst ..	11 22	2 29		
Woolston .. ,,		2 29	4 47	Southampton West ..	11 45	2 54		
St. Denys .. ,,		2 37	4 53	St. Denys ..				
Southampton West .. ,,	11 9	1 50	5 0	Woolston ..				
Brockenhurst .. ,,	11 36		5 35	Netley ..		3 10		
Christchurch .. ,,	11 56		6 15	Fareham .. ,,	12 22			
Pokesdown .. ,,	12 2			Portsmouth and				
Boscombe .. ,,	12 5		6 23	Southsea .. .. arr	12 47			
Bournemouth { Central. ,,	12 10		6 29					
{ West .. ,,	12 24		6 43	Fareham .. .. dep	12 14	3 29	4 12	
				Chichester .. .. arr	12 50	3 57	4 41	
				Bognor .. ,,	1 25	4 39	5 7	
Fareham .. .. dep		1 32		Littlehampton .. ,,	1 20	4 45	5 37	
Salisbury .. .. arr	12 40	2 35		Arundel .. ,,	1 37	4 53	5 35	
Lyme Regis .. ,,	3 32	5 4		Worthing .. ,,	1 16	4 22	5 10	
Seaton .. ,,	3 38	5 2		Hove .. ,,	1 32	4 40	5 28	
Sidmouth .. ,,	3 4	5 38		Brighton .. ,,	1 37	4 45	5 33	
Exeter (Queen Street) .. ,,	2 41	4 37						
Exeter (St. David's) .. ,,	2 53	4 46						
Barnstaple Junction .. ,,	5 46	5 59		Lewes .. .. arr	2 10	5 25	6 1	
Bideford .. ,,		6 20		Newhaven Harbour ,,	2 50	5 47	6 26	
Torrington .. ,,		6 31		Seaford .. ,,	2 57	5 53	6 33	
Ilfracombe .. ,,		6 54		Eastbourne .. ,,	2 50	5 33	6 30	
Bude .. ,,	5 24	6 52		Bexhill Central .. ,,	2 6	6 14	6 56	
Wadebridge .. ,,	6 21	9 24		St. Leonards (W. M.) ,,	3 12	6 21	7 5	
Padstow .. ,,	6 40	9 42		St. Leonards (W. Sq.) ,,	3 16	6 26	7 10	
Plymouth (North Road). ,,	4 37	6 30		Hastings .. ,,	3 20	6 30	7 14	

A 10 50 a.m. on Sats.   B 11 29 a.m. on Sats.   C Leaves Bognor on Saturdays at 2 20 p.m.

1924

PORTSMOUTH HARBOUR

1. Between 1840 and 1847 intending railway passengers in Portsmouth were obliged to cross the Harbour by ferry to Gosport to join a train. A steam operated chain ferry commenced operation in 1840 and this illustra-

tion shows the fourth and final vessel on the route, the *Duchess of York*, at Gosport. It was built in 1892 and served until the service ceased in 1959. (Hampshire County Museum Service)

This map shows the original layout of the station which was opened on 2nd October 1876. Until then, passengers had to pass

through the streets of the city between their train and ferry journeys.

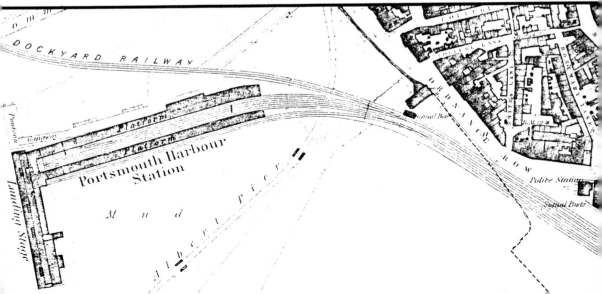

2. Looking north from the Harbour Station we can see coaches standing on the South Jetty line and the signalling tower in the background. This had been erected to send messages to the Admiralty in London by means of a series of 17 hilltop semaphore signalling stations. The system became redundant with the coming of the railways, as their lineside electric telegraph was quicker and not dependent on clear visibility.
(Hampshire County Library)

3. Two additional platforms were added onto the south side of the original three and were brought into use on 13th July 1903. One of the class C8 LSWR 4-4-0s awaits departure north, revealing the clean lines achieved by its designer, Dugald Drummond, by having inside cylinders and inside bearings.
(National Railway Museum)

4. The station was substantially rebuilt and the platforms lengthened prior to electrification, although the number of platforms remained unaltered. This view shows an early stage of the work on 6th March 1937. (C.E.C. Townsend)

London Brighton & South Coast Railway.

Henfield to

Portsm'th Har.

London and South Western Ry.

787

From _____

TO

Portsmouth Harbour

5. In 1940-41, the station was almost totally destroyed by enemy bombing although access to part of Platform 1 and the Gun Wharf siding was possible after extensive repairs. This July 1970 photograph shows the station as rebuilt in 1946; D7037 at the head of a Bristol train and the banner repeater signal indicating imminent departure of a fast train to Waterloo. (J. Scrace)

6. The line to the Gun Wharf once descended the ramp on the right. It was out of use in the early 1930s but saw much activity during WWII and was finally removed in 1955. The unusual electric locomotive is *Sarah Siddons*, built for the Metropolitan Railway in 1922, seen here arriving with *The Mary Rose* rail-tour on 7th July 1984. (D. Fereday Glenn)

PORTSMOUTH TOWN STATION.

7. The elegant buildings date from 1866. A goods line to the Dockyard crossed the road on the level until the high level platforms were built in 1876. The original station had been built just outside the "Inner Defences", a wall built to protect Portsmouth from landward invasion. (Lens of Sutton)

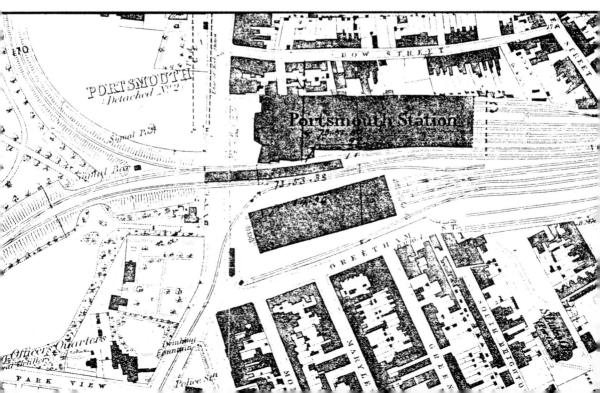

8. The name "Portsmouth Town" was in use between 1876 and 1921, although modern road signs nearby confirm that this name continues to be used locally. The entire roof survives today but the site of platforms 1 to 4 became a car park for a DIY store in 1985. (Lens of Sutton)

An interesting feature of this 1882 map is the street tramway running into the goods yard from Southsea Pier. It was horse worked and formed the nucleus of the subsequent Corporation Tramways. On the right is the four-road locomotive shed, superseded in 1889 by a larger shed at Fratton. On the left are the lines to the Harbour and at the top is the single line to the North Dockyard.

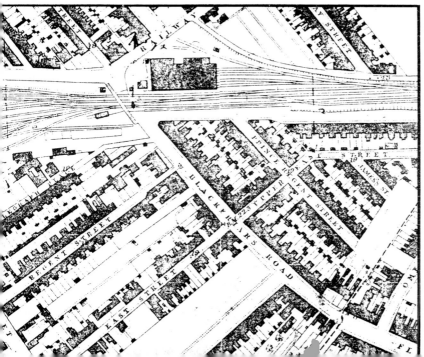

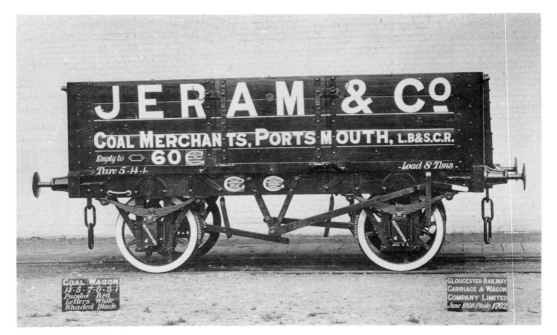

9. Prior to nationalisation, most coal merchants provided their own coal wagons but during WWII their identification became difficult as broken boards were replaced and not relettered. This builders photograph carries every detail of their fine product. (Historic Model Railway Society)

The 1898 edition reveals the loss of the wagon turn plates at each end of the goods shed and the provision of a larger locomotive turntable.

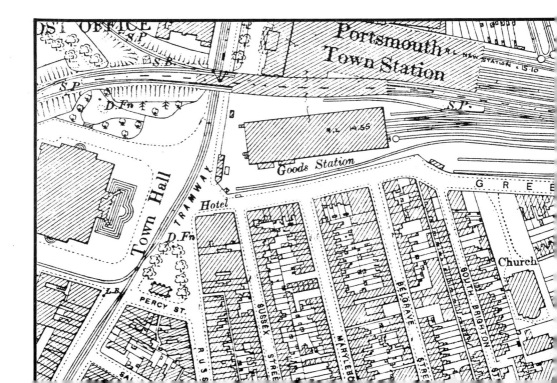

10. Heavy bombing on 3rd May 1941 caused serious disruption to the railway. An EMU wrecked in the berthing sidings adjacent to the high-level lines is seen here being cut up, after removal of usable fittings. The full story of the SR in WWII is told vividly in *War on the Line* (Middleton Press). (British Rail)

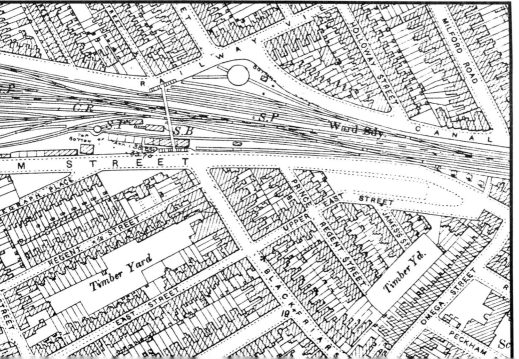

11. A busy scene on 14th October 1954. Battle of Britain class *601 Squadron* no.34071 waits in the foreground as standby engine for the Emperor of Ethiopia's Pullman train. Behind it, one of the Brighton Belle electric sets runs down the 1 in 61 gradient from the high level platforms, bound for Victoria with guests. (E.W. Fry)

12. Looking north from platform 5 in June 1955, we see one of the remaining class T9s hauling a rake of Maunsell designed coaches under the footbridge known as Jacob's Ladder. (P. Hay)

13. A vacuum braked class O2 (fitted with air operated push-pull equipment) ascends the incline to platform 6 on 8th April 1957, travelling "wrong line" in order to reach the North Dockyard line, which diverged near the west end of this platform. (D. Fereday Glenn)

14. A "cross-country" DMU leaves the high-level at 11.09 on 7th September 1966, bound for Cardiff. These units were poor time keepers and were transferred to Scotland two years later. The 11.15 departure for Plymouth stands at platform 4, headed by 2–6–0 class 4 no. 76058. This train would wait at Fareham for 20 minutes to be coupled to the Brighton portion. (J. Scrace)

FRATTON

15. The station and the branch to East Southsea were both opened on 1st July 1885. Terrier no. 48 is seen at the branch platform. Note the enormous wooden brake blocks and the slot in the signal post in the background. (E.R. Lacey collection)

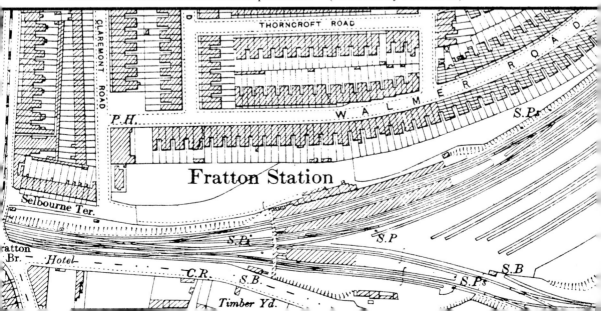

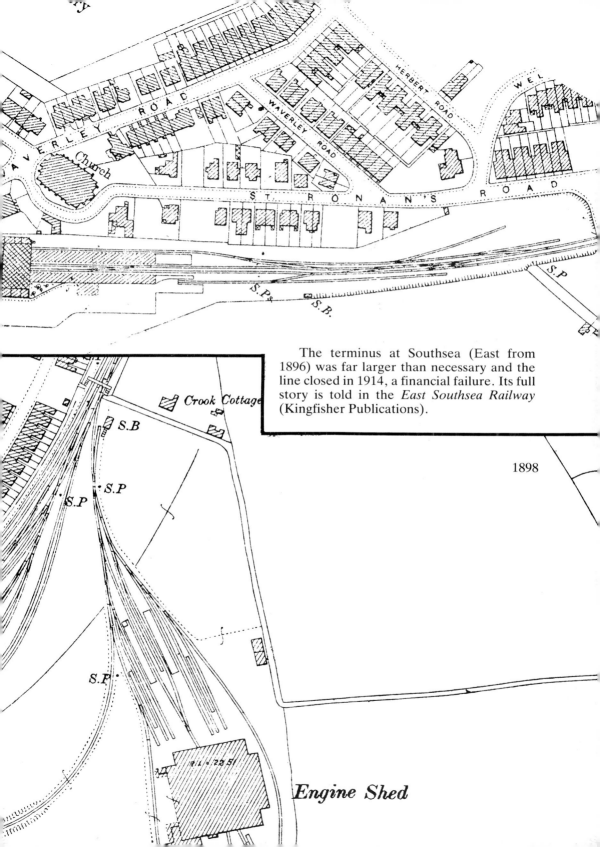

The terminus at Southsea (East from 1896) was far larger than necessary and the line closed in 1914, a financial failure. Its full story is told in the *East Southsea Railway* (Kingfisher Publications).

1898

16. A new locomotive shed was planned in 1889 and was shared by the LSWR & LBSCR but each company had its own offices. This view shows the 50ft. turntable and the gloomy atmosphere in October 1933. (W. Bishop)

17. U class 2–6–0 no. 31807 arrives with a train from Fareham in 1952. The station was known as Fratton & Southsea between 1905 and 1921. The fine tracery in the canopy brackets survives today. (J.A.G. Coltas)

18. BR standard class 4 no. 76006 attracts admirers as it proceeds north with the 12.45 Plymouth train on 3rd November 1963. The merit of tall signal posts is evident in this view. (E. Wilmshurst)

19. An eastward view from the footbridge in 1966 shows the level crossing gates and yard ground frame, between the carriage shed and the washer. The crossing only gave access to the yard and was closed in 1969. This was the site of the East Southsea branch platforms. (D. Cullum)

20. On 7th April 1968, Portsmouth Panel Box displaced Fratton West and Fratton East boxes. The box seen in the previous photograph was replaced by a new ground frame, close to the washing plant, at the same time. (J. Scrace)

A map adapted by German spies in 1939 indicates the railway layout at the gasworks and the War Department Depot – both key targets. Eastern Road was then under construction but the words Straße im Bau were wrongly placed by the railway! This is reproduced from *Battle over Portsmouth* (Middleton Press).

21. D7031 approaches with the 9.20 Portsmouth Harbour to Bristol service on 7th July 1970. The railway from this point to Portsmouth & Southsea was built on the route of the former Portsmouth Canal and the buildings on the right were provided for railway staff. (J. Scrace)

Portsmouth-Hilsea
Heereszeugamt
Länge (westl. Greenw.): 1° 3' 30" Breite: 50° 49' 50"
Mißweisung: -11° (Mitte 1939)

1:63360 Bl. Nr. 132
1:100000 Bl. Nr. 38

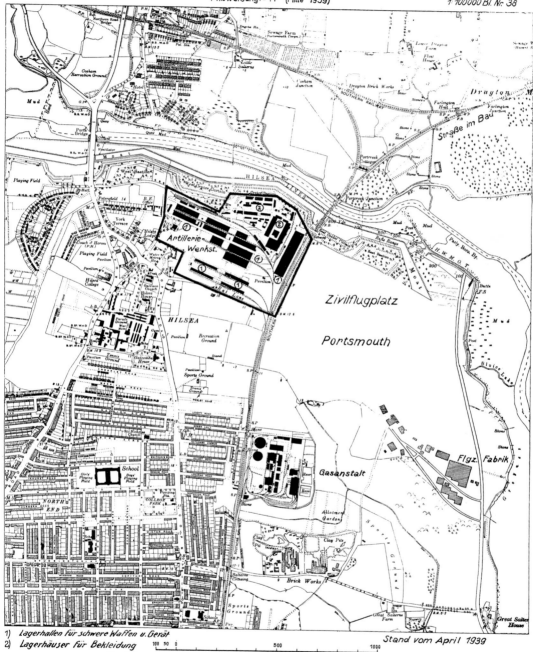

1) Lagerhallen für schwere Waffen u. Gerät
2) Lagerhäuser für Bekleidung
     u. Ausrüstung

Stand vom April 1939

100 50 0   500   1000

Maßstab 1:10 560

HILSEA

22. After ceasing coal gas production, Hilsea Works produced methane ("natural gas") from naphtha, a petroleum by-product. This 1961 Ruston diesel shunter (no. 463153) was used for moving naphtha tank wagons until 1985. The sidings were lifted early in 1986. (V. Mitchell)

24. The inner defences of Portsmouth prevented the railway builders reaching the waterfront – the outer defences (the Hilsea Lines – see map) were penetrated by a short "tunnel". A 4CIG unit is passing through it in the background whilst no. 33033 speeds south with a train from Cardiff on 17th April 1982. (J.S. Petley)

Other views and maps of the locations described in this album so far can be seen in our companion albums *Chichester to Portsmouth* and *Woking to Portsmouth*. Further photographs of the area are included in *Steaming through East Hants*.

23. The halt was opened 2nd November 1941 to bring workers to the Admiralty factory and to those on the nearby airfield. The entire structure and fittings were pre-fabricated at the SR's Exmouth Junction concrete works. (Lens of Sutton)

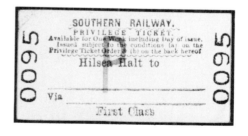

SOUTHERN RAILWAY.
PRIVILEGE TICKET.
Available for One Week including Day of issue.
Issued subject to the conditions (a) on the
Privilege Ticket Order 8 (b) on the back hereof
Hilsea Halt to

Via

First Class

0095   0095

25. Portsmouth had for long feared an attack from its hinterland and in addition to its inner and outer defences it had the benefit of the natural barrier of Portcreek. To maintain this security, the railway was obliged to provide this drawbridge. (Portsmouth City Record Office)

26. Cosham Junction is at the western end of the triangular junction and was controlled by this signal box until 5th May 1968. The DEMU formed the stopping train from Salisbury, three days before the box closed. The distant signals were worked by the next boxes east and south. (J. Scrace)

COSHAM

27. World events were sometimes reflected at the local goods yard. Here troops gather with their equipment ready for departure to the Boer War. Until 1966, there were also single sidings south east, south west and north west of the station. (E.V. Bugden collection)

The 1876 map shows fields separating the station from the village and a pound for stray animals. The LBSCR operated freight to Cosham from 26th July 1848 and LSWR trains started running to Portsmouth on 1st October 1848. For many years the LBSCR operated a shuttle service to Havant from the down bay platform but the line to Portsmouth was jointly operated by a management committee.

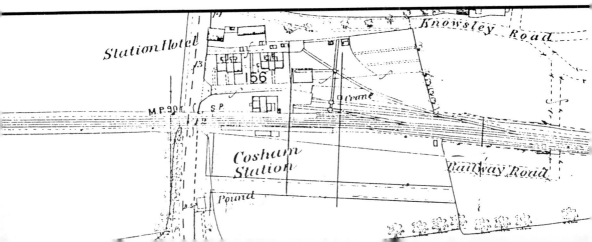

28. The rural view, looking north around the turn of the century, reveals the tramway terminus in the foreground. (E.V. Bugden collection)

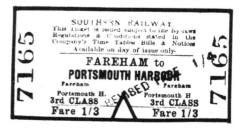

29. Yet further defences were erected in WWII in the form of concrete cubes alongside the railway to impede enemy movement following an invasion. Class D15 no. 30466 departs for Fareham with some GWR coaches, passing these long forgotten objects. (D. Cullum collection)

30. Looking towards Fareham, on 9th May 1980, we see the down side buildings on the right. The goods shed was originally behind this but in 1935 it was demolished and a new one was built further north. The yard closed in June 1970. (J. Scrace)

31. Moving to the footbridge on the same day, we gain a closer look at the signal box, which closed in June 1982. An overbridge was erected in 1925 for the Cosham bypass and until 1935 the trams of the Portsdown & Horndean Light Railway also crossed on an overbridge here. (J. Scrace)

32. The two-room up side building probably dates from the opening of the line. The western wooden canopy stanchion has been replaced by a bent bullhead rail. Colour light signals were introduced here in 1968. (V. Mitchell)

PAULSGROVE HALT

33. Between 1933 and 1939 this halt was in use on race days. It was 1¼ miles west of Cosham station. (Lens of Sutton)

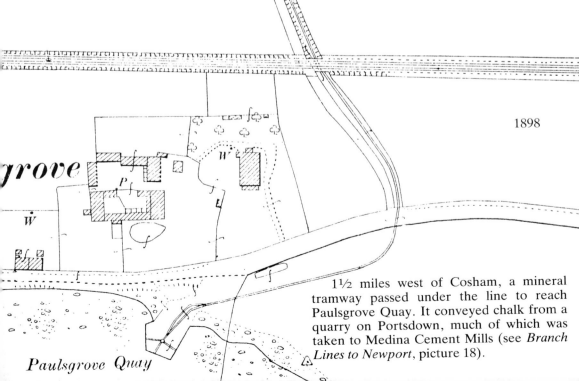

grove

1898

Paulsgrove Quay

1½ miles west of Cosham, a mineral tramway passed under the line to reach Paulsgrove Quay. It conveyed chalk from a quarry on Portsdown, much of which was taken to Medina Cement Mills (see *Branch Lines to Newport*, picture 18).

34. Situated on an embankment, the station was opened on 1st September 1848, when services commenced from Fareham as far as Cosham. The up side building is unusual, being built of local flints, with brick quoins and fitted with assorted chimney pots. (Lens of Sutton)

35. As its name implies, the place has Roman nautical origins. Its fine castle is neglected by many modern tourists but no doubt has generated much passenger traffic here in times past, when our ancestors would not think twice of walking nearly a mile from the station. (Lens of Sutton)

In 1897, the station was remote from the village.

S.P

S.P

S.P

S.B.   L.B

Portchester Station

E S T E

Port

W

Pound

P

J.

W

Smy

P

Hotel

P

L.B

W

W

P

W's

P

10·3

Drill Hall

Tobaccopipe Manufact

P

W

P

School

Brewery

P

P

FAREHAM

36. On the misty morning of Saturday 19th October 1967, the 00.30 Colwick to Fawley tank train crosses the Wallington Viaduct on the outskirts of the town. It had been diverted from the main line because of bridge works at Winchester Junction. (J.H. Bird)

1898

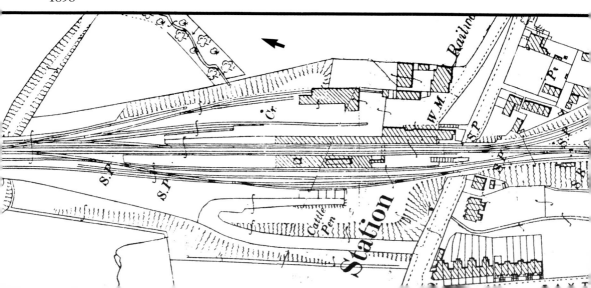

37. For many decades, trains from the west were divided here, the larger Brighton portion leaving first. This is the Portsmouth section of a train from Cardiff leaving at 5.10pm on 26th August 1960 behind Q class no. 30536, an engine more commonly seen on freight services. (D. Fereday Glenn)

38. An unusual train on 20th March 1966 was the Southampton Docks to Waterloo boat train powered by BR standard class 5 no. 73114 and diverted via Havant due to electrification work on the direct line. The roof of the large goods shed can be seen in the background. (L. Elsey)

39. Diesel no. 33019 runs light through the down platform on 21st July 1976 as the 15.28 Fareham to Eastleigh waits in the centre road for the 14.56 Portsmouth Harbour to Bristol to arrive. The goods shed on the left closed in 1970 but much of the goods yard remains in use as a stone terminal for limestone road material from Foster Yeoman's Merehead Quarry in the Mendips. (J. Scrace)

40. In 1971, the former up main line was truncated to form a bay for the Eastleigh shuttle service. This permitted realignment of the road bridge at the southern approach to the station to ease the severity of the curve. (Lens of Sutton)

41. Looking east along the original main line from the home signal in 1928, we see the direct Botley line in the foreground; the Knowle Tunnel diversion branching from it and the Southampton line on the right. The story of the tunnel and the diversion is told in our *Branch Lines to Alton*. (Late E. Wallis)

42. Class Q1 no. 33005 departs for Eastleigh with its lengthy freight train from Chichester, on 24th June 1950. Behind it is East Box, which was at the north end of the station and slightly west of West Box. Railwaymen were never confused as the East Box was always nearer to London, when viewed from the LSWR route. (D. Cullum)

SWANWICK

43. This post card view impresses on one the rural location of the station and the correct pronunciation. The house lost its foliage and projecting brickwork some years ago and is now a licensed restaurant – the "Strawberries and Steam". (D. Cullum collection)

44. At the east end, a ground frame gave access to the goods yard. Passing it on the last day of 1955 is class T9 no. 30702, bound for Bournemouth West. (D. Cullum)

45. Week-end diversions were frequent in 1965-66. This is the 11.30 Waterloo to Bournemouth West on 25th April 1965, hauled by no. 34022 *Exmoor* and is about to pass under the B3051, the road to Botley. (J. Scrace)

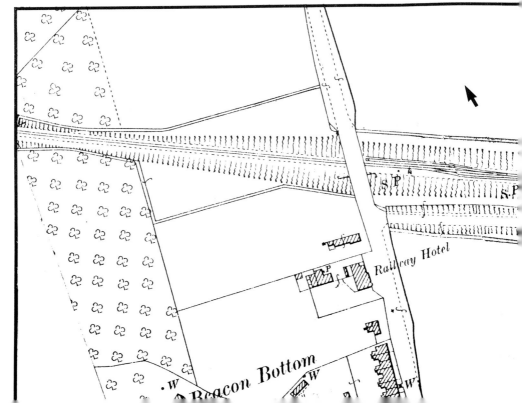

46. The goods yard was extended in 1896, altered again in 1951 and closed on 4th January 1965. It despatched vast tonnages of strawberries in the season and this continued until 1966. In October 1967, the yard was again remodelled for the reception of power station fly ash for a nearby building block manufacturer. The traffic was short lived and the tracks were lifted in 1972. Another diverted train is seen, bound for Waterloo on 20th March 1966, behind no. 34024 *Tamar Valley*. (J. Scrace)

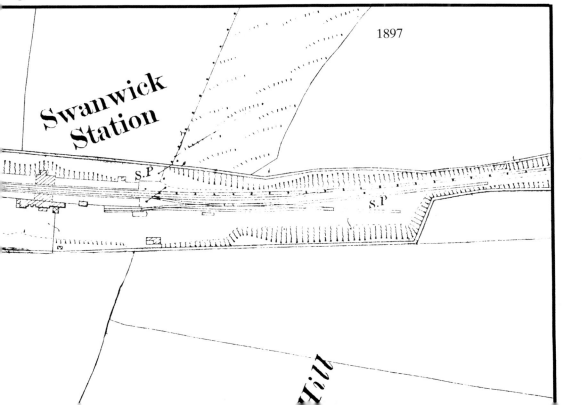

47. Until 1951, a siding was provided between the down platform (on the right) and the road bridge. The signal box closed on 9th March 1980, although the ground frame had been closed in 1967. (J. Scrace)

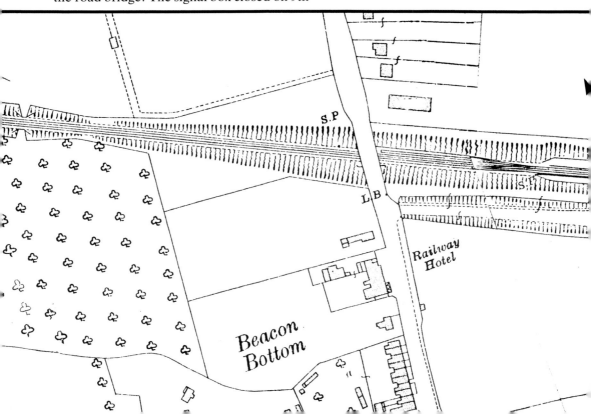

48. The house and station were built to the same design as those at Worplesdon and in the same decade. By 1986, the booking hall had lost its dummy dormer windows but the office was still staffed. (J. Scrace)

1932

Swanwick Station

S.P

S.B.   S.P   Cr

50. No. 31420 passes the site of the down siding on 5th April 1980, whilst speeding west with a Cardiff train. Parts of the goods yard had more colourful names – the crossover was *Squint Eye* and the extension of the back siding was *Spion Cop*. (J. Scrace)

←

49. To improve visibility the Down Home signal was suspended from "gallows". By the time this photograph was taken in 1978, the Up Starter had lost its high level co-acting arm but both signals retained their LSWR lattice posts. (J. Scrace)

London Brighton & South Coast Railway.

West Worthing to

BOURNEMOUTH WEST

(L. & S.W.R., via *FRATTON*)

BURSLEDON

51. The line was not doubled until 1910 although the civil engineering structures allowed for two tracks to be laid. The steep hillside prevented more than two sidings being provided although a short headshunt and a crossover were added after doubling. Don't miss the elegant steam launch and the delicate road bridge. (Lens of Sutton)

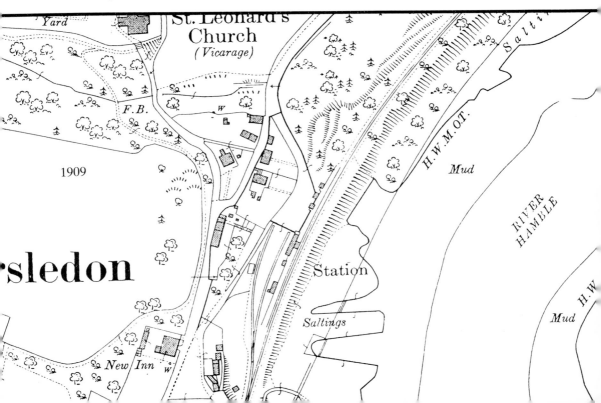

52. A class A12 arrives from Netley and passes the small goods yard ground frame box. Two ladders seem excessive for tending five oil lights. (Lens of Sutton)

53. A Portsmouth to Ilfracombe train rumbles slowly over the Hamble River on 10th August 1957. Moguls and "Schools" were restricted to 20mph on the bridge. ½ mile to the east, a siding was provided for the Bursledon Brick Co. between 1898 and 1961 on the down side and Crow Park Halt was in use on the up side only from 1918 to about 1920. (E. Wilmshurst)

54. Many strawberry specials were run to various parts of the country. This is the Swanwick to Southampton service on 21st June 1961, hauled by Q class no. 30535. The massive road bridge serves only a few waterfront houses. (D. Fereday Glenn)

55. The goods yard closed in 1960; the station became unstaffed in 1968; the building was demolished in 1969; the signal box closed in 1980 but fortunately trains still call once an hour. (J. Scrace)

56. On 18th April 1970, a mechanical digger travelling on a lorry struck the bridge, despite 16 feet of headroom. The damage necessitated single line working and closure of the road. No. 34040 *Crewkerne* passes over with the diverted "Bournemouth Belle" on 25th April 1965. (J. Scrace)

57. The signal box was provided when the route was doubled in 1910 and ceased to be required on 27th June 1961. New colour light signalling was brought into use on 9th March 1980 but the gas lights had been modernised some years earlier. (J. Scrace)

58. Nos. 33001 and 33033 double head the 08.53 Brighton to Exeter St. Davids service on 22nd July 1978, which ran on Saturdays only. The proliferation of pleasure boating makes an interesting comparison with the earlier photographs (J. Scrace)

HAMBLE

59. As at Hilsea, an all-concrete pre-fabricated structure was erected during WWII, although the footbridge is of steel construction and was probably erected later. Services commenced on 18th January 1942 and were largely for the benefit of those working at the three aircraft factories nearby. Between 1930 and 1961, there had been a siding east of the halt on the down side for Sandells' Loam and Gravel Co. (J. Scrace)

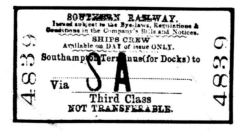

60. A few yards west of the halt a private line commences to the BP Oil Terminal. It is protected by two gates between which the footpath (on the right) passes. Beyond the gates, the track splits into three roads – reception, desptach and run round. No. D6578 removes loaded tankers on 6th September 1967, whilst the brake van stands on the up line. (J.H. Bird)

62. The line crosses the road to Hamble twice and is here guarded by unusual gates, part of which also swings across the footway.

This is a northward view at the first crossing. (J.H. Bird)

←

61. On 22nd March 1975, there was a very rare visit of a passenger train – a Branch line Society railtour. DEMU no. 1124 proceeds

past the ground frame which by 1986 was devoid of a building. (J.H. Bird)

Bradshaw 1890

Fares.			Dock Station.	urn	mrn	mrn	aft	aft	aft	aft		mrn	mrn	mrn	non	aft	aft	aft	aft
1 cl.	2 cl.	3 cl.	**Southampton** dep	7	0	9 15	1015	1220	1 40	3 55	5 53	8 15	**Portsmouth Town**	7 20	8 45	....	12 0	....	3 35	5 25	7 53
s.d.	s.d.	s.d.	Northam	7	3	9 18	1018	1223	1 43	3 58	5 56	8 18	Fratton 50	7 23	8 48	....	12 3	....	3 38	....	7 56
0 4	0 3	0 2	St. Denys	7	7	9 21	1022	1227	1 47	4 2	5 59	8 22	Cosham	7 32	8 56	....	1212	....	3 47	....	8 5
0 10	0 40	0 2½	Bitterne Road	7 10	9 23	1025	1230	1 50	4 5	6 3	5 25		Porchester	7 34	9 3	....	1219	....	3 54	....	8 12
0 7	0 50	0 4	Woolston	7 16	....	1031	1236	1 51	4 11	6 7	8 31	Fareham..........	7 47	9 10	....	1227	....	4 2	5 41	8 20
0 10	0 70	0 5	Sholing	7 19	....	1034	1239	1 57	4 14	6 10	8 34	Swanwick	7 55	9 17	....	1232	2 25	4 10	....	8 2
1 00	1 90	0 6½	Netley	7 26	9 33	1039	1247	2 3	4 22	6 16	8 40	Bursledon	8 1	9 23	....	1241	2 31	4 16	....	8 24
....	....	....	Bursledon	7 32	....	....	1253	2 9	4 28	6 22	8 46	Netley	8 10	9 32	1045	1250	2 38	4 25	5 56	5 41
....	....	....	Swanwick	7 38	....	....	1259	2 15	4 34	6 28	8 52	Sholing	8 15	....	1050	1255	2 43	4 30	....	8 46
....	....	....	Fareham (above).	7 47	9 48	....	1 8	....	4 45	6 39	9 1	Woolston	8 18	9 38	1053	1258	2 46	4 33	....	8 49
....	....	....	Porchester	7 54	....	....	1 16	....	4 40	....	9 8	Bitterne Road....	8 22	9 44	105	1 3	2 50	4 38	6 3	8 54
....	....	....	Cosham 64	8 1	....	....	1 25	....	4 56	6 46	9 15	St. Denys 45....	8 27	9 47	11 5	1 7	2 53	4 42	6 5	8 58
....	....	....	Fratton 50, 53, 70	8 10	10 3	....	1 34	....	5 9	6 59	9 24	Northam	8 31	9 50	11 6	1 11	2 57	4 46	6 8	9 2
....	....	....	Portsmouth Town	8 13	10 5	....	1 37	....	5 6	5 59	9 27	SouthamptonDks.	8 35	9 53	1110	1 13	3 0	4 50	6 10	9 6

SOUTHAMPTON, NETLEY, FAREHAM, and PORTSMOUTH.—London and South Western.

63. The same train is seen standing at the side of the Hamble Airfield, looking some-what lost on unfenced track. (J.H. Bird)

64. The terminal has a pier into South-ampton Water at which a wide variety of petroleum products were off-loaded from coastal shipping for distribution. This Sep-tember 1967 view shows BP's nearly new Hunslet 0–6–0 Diesel hauling bitumen tankers (J.H. Bird)

65. Earlier, motive power had been supplied by Hundswell no. 21, seen here returning light into the depot and about to pass under an unusual steel footbridge. The speed limit referred to the road. (D. Fereday Glenn)

66. On 26th July 1985, a test train was run to the oil terminal to establish the feasibility of using BR diesel electric locomotives to haul train loads of crude oil from the Dorset oilfields. A class 73 worked at each end of the 10 bogie tankers for the trial. Subsequently a BR class 08 regularly operated the train on the branch, until November 1985 after which the oil went direct to the Esso refinery at Fawley. (J.R. Fairman)

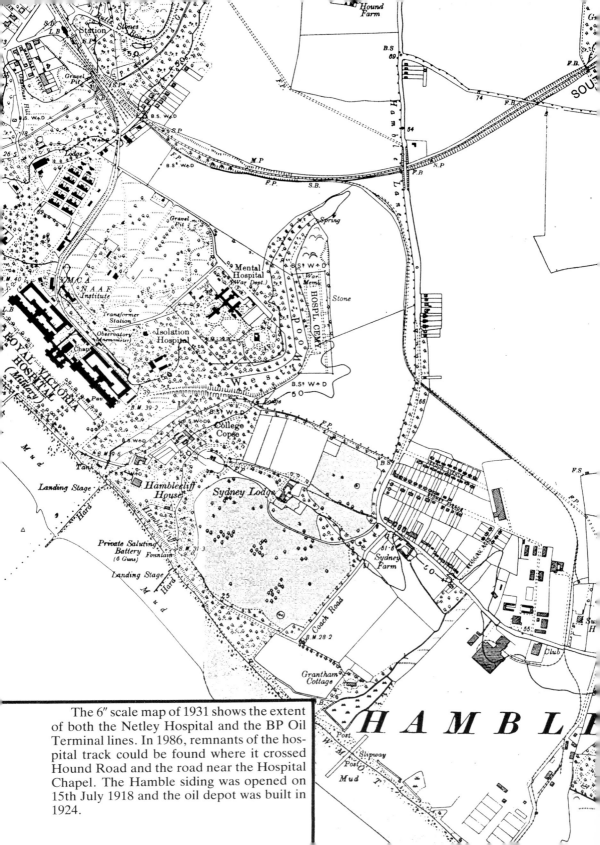

The 6″ scale map of 1931 shows the extent of both the Netley Hospital and the BP Oil Terminal lines. In 1986, remnants of the hospital track could be found where it crossed Hound Road and the road near the Hospital Chapel. The Hamble siding was opened on 15th July 1918 and the oil depot was built in 1924.

NETLEY

67. An early postcard view shows the small building on the down side which appears to date from the opening of the line and remarkably still survives in 1986. (Lens of Sutton)

68. The 3.40 pm Portsmouth & Southsea to Salisbury service collects a few passengers on Sunday 7th July 1957. The dock siding to the right of the railings was provided from the outset and survived until 1964. The locomotive is a 2–6–0, one of the BR standard class 4s. (P. Hay)

69. Class 4 no. 75065 pauses at the down platform with a van train on 25th July 1963. The entrance to the goods yard is in the foreground. At the end of the yard, a platform was provided for patients of Netley Hospital and this was supplied with a waiting room in 1899. On 18th April 1900, a line direct to the hospital was opened, built at a cost of £4090 and paid for by the Government. (J. Scrace)

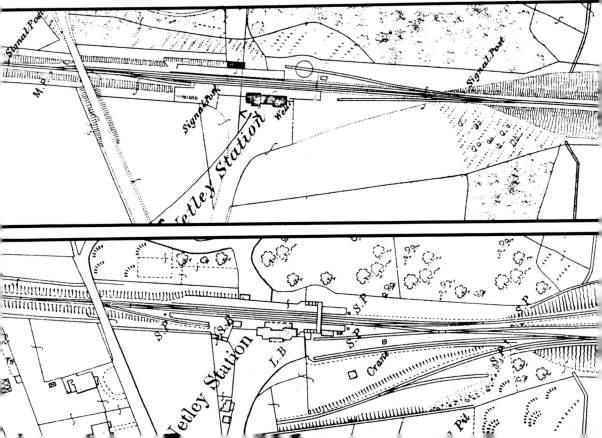

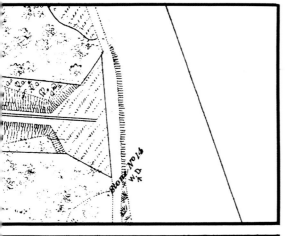

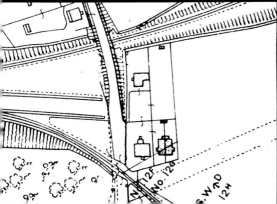

70. The signal box ceased to be used with the introduction of colour light signals on 9th March 1980. It was subsequently dismantled and re-erected at Ropley on the Mid-Hants Railway, once again to control the movement of steam locomotives. (J. Scrace)

⬅

The 1866 map shows the station as a terminus, complete with a small turntable. The line terminated in straight track, from which it was originally intended to extend direct to Hamble village.

⬅

The 1909 edition shows the Fareham line diverging (top right) and the Netley Hospital line (lower right). Part of the latter was still visible in the road at the level crossing in 1986.

71. The fine building is now "Listed Grade 2" and is described as stuccoed brick with rusticated quoins, in Victorian Italianate style. Woolston and St. Denys stations are in similar style and also Listed. Until 1905, it had a Tea Bar and in 1986, it was awaiting tenants for the empty upper floor. (J. Scrace)

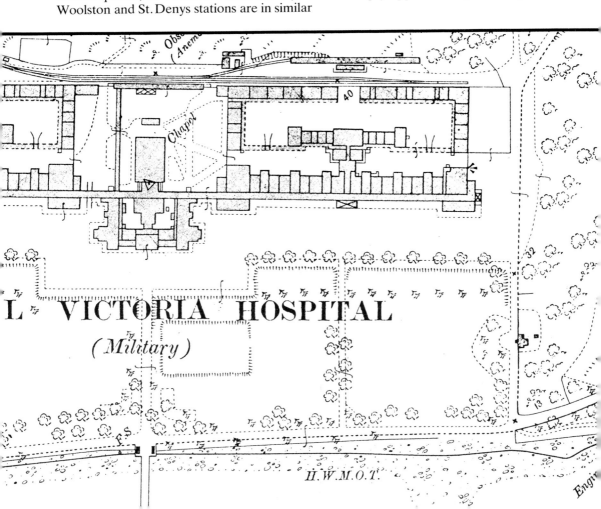

72. The Netley Hospital branch Home signal stood surrounded by weeds in July 1963, the year in which the line officially closed, although the last train had left on 30th August 1955! Further details can be found in *Netley Hospital and its Railways* (Kingfisher Publications).

All but the Chapel was demolished in 1967 and this now stands isolated in a public park. The platform was immediately behind it and had an awning for its full length. The long narrow building could house four ward cars and was removed to the Longmoor Military Railway in 1957.

SHOLING

73. This was the only station on the Netley branch not to be provided with substantial buildings. It was opened on 1st August 1866. The originals were replaced by the present structures in 1910 which became unstaffed in December 1965. For sometime thereafter, the nearby newsagent sold railway tickets. (J. Scrace)

74. The 13.35 Portsmouth & Southsea to Southampton DEMU calls on 25th July 1972, the date of the previous photograph also. A coal siding was provided here prior to the doubling of the line. (J. Scrace)

WOOLSTON

75. Looking west from the road bridge, we can see the reverse curves of the main line which resulted from the route curving shar-ply from Southampton Water to the Itchen Valley. Note the small wooden goods shed. (Lens of Sutton)

1881 – single line with loop and one siding.

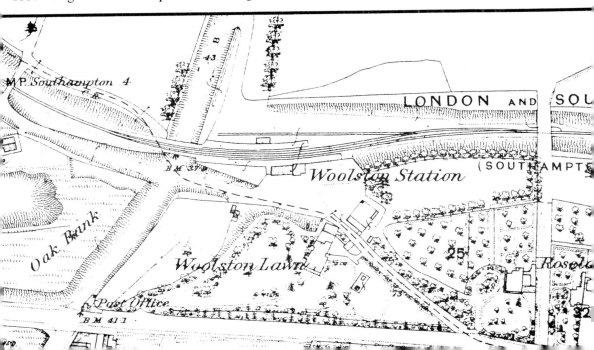

76. *Wadebridge* heads an empty tank train from Hamble to Stanlow on 24th August 1965. The goods yard closed in November 1967 and ironically became the home of a road transport firm with the railway-sounding title of Solent Express. (J.H. Bird)

1897 – single line but with the loop disconnected, an additional siding and land marked as purchased (for goods yard expansion). The loop was reinstated in 1901.

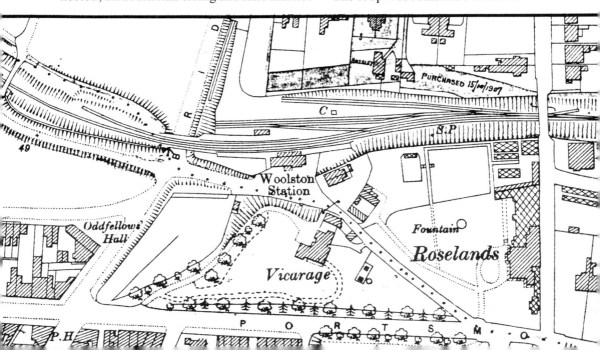

77. The south facade is seen in June 1976, during the extensive road alterations. On the left is the massive ventilator of the Gents and on the right is the back of the signal box. This was opened in 1901, closed in 1980 and still remained in position in 1986. (J. Scrace)

1933 – goods yard fully developed including a new goods shed.

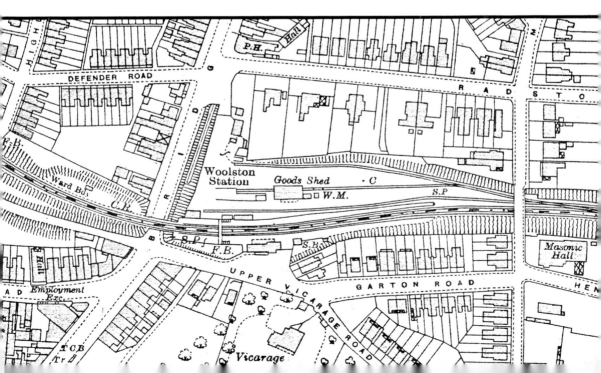

78. A roof-boarded Cardiff to Portsmouth train begins the 1 in 80 climb from the river shore, on the left, to Woolston on 21st April 1956. Between the embankment and the hillside the Chief Civil Engineer has tipped waste materials and sidings were in place for this purpose between 1954 and 1976. The locomotive is a BR standard class 4 and is seen again at Southampton Terminus. (L. Elsey)

1933

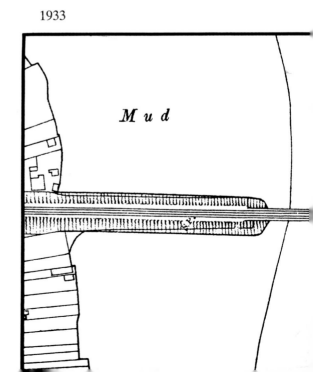

BITTERNE

79. Known as Bitterne Road until 1896, the station is adjacent to the main road to Southampton via Northam Bridge. Improvements to this road have necessitated the widening of the bridge over the railway in 1910 and again in 1931–32. The footbridge was erected in 1903. (D. Cullum)

80. In 1986 the buildings remained unaltered, the house being occupied by a medical company. The goods yard was closed as early as 1959 and the signal box in 1966. Both photographs were taken in the following year. (D. Cullum)

81. From Bitterne the line runs almost north, crosses the River Itchen and then curves sharply south to cross Adelaide Road on the level, as it approaches St. Denys. Here we look north in May 1966, a month before the crossing gates were replaced by lifting barriers. The box ceased to function in October 1981, when CCTV was installed. (D. Cullum)

SOUTHERN RAILWAY

CHEAP "MONTHLY RETURN" TICKETS
From Portsmouth and Fratton

ANY DAY—ANY TRAIN—ANYWHERE
(except "Zoo" and "Continental Boat" Trains)

Forward or Return—ANY DAY WITHIN ONE MONTH
(Except Sundays)

WITH BREAK OF JOURNEY AT ANY INTERMEDIATE STATION

Minimum Fares:—1st Class 7 6, 3rd Class 5 -

To	Return Fares 3rd Class from Portsmouth & Southsea	Fratton	To	Return Fares 3rd Class from Portsmouth & Southsea	Fratton
ABERDEEN	99 8	99 9	LIVERPOOL	62	62
ANDOVER TOWN	8 5	8 7	LLANDUDNO	47 3	47 3
ASHFORD (Kent) (B)	18 11	18 8	LONDON	13 2	12 10
AXMINSTER	18 11	18 8	LYME REGIS	19 11	19 11
BARNSTAPLE	27 4	27	LYMINGTON TOWN	7 11	7 7
BASINGSTOKE	8 5	8 5	LYNTON	29 3	19 11
BENTALL CENTRAL	13 2	13 2	MAIDSTONE WEST (C)	16 10	16 10
BIDEFORD	28 11	28 11	MANCHESTER	40 5	40 5
BIRMINGHAM	26 3	26 3	MARGATE (A)	25 9	25 6
BLACKPOOL	47 3	47 3	NEWCASTLE-ON-TYNE	59 7	59 7
BOGNOR REGIS	5	5	NEWHAVEN TOWN (C)	10 6	10 3
BOSCOMBE	9 5	9 2	NEWPORT I.W. (D)	5	5
BOURNEMOUTH CENTRAL	9 5	9 5	NORWICH	33 4	33 1
BRIGHTON	7 2	7 11	ORAN	97 5	97 5
BRISTOL	17 4	17 4	OKEHAMPTON	22 3	22 10
BRIMSDOWN (A)	26 3	26	PADSTOW	38 1	37 10
BRACKNELL	6 10	6 10	PLYMOUTH	22 10	22 7
BUDE	33 4	33 1	PORTSMOUTH	2	2
CANTERBURY WEST (B)	21	21	POOLE	10 6	10 6
CARDIFF	25 2	25 2	PORTLAND	16 3	16 3
CARLISLE	62 3	62 3	RAMSGATE (A)	26 6	26 3
CHARD	18 8	18 5	READING (via Guildford)	11	11
CHATHAM (A)	18 8	18 5	ROCHESTER (A)	18 8	18 5
CHRISTCHURCH	8 11	8 11	RYE (B)	16	15 9
COWES, I.W. (D)	5	5	ST. LEONARDS (C)	13 11	13 8
DEAL (B)	23 11	23 11	SALISBURY	8 2	8 2
DEVONPORT	22 10	22 7	SANDWICH (B)	23 11	23 11
DORCHESTER	14 5	14 5	SCARBOROUGH	52 6	52 6
DOUGLAS, I. of M. (via Liverpool and I. of M. S.P. Co.)	55	55	STAFFORD (C)	18 10	18 10
DOVER (B)	22 6	22 1	SLAPTON	29 3	19 11
DUNDEE	89 3	89 3	SHANKLIN, I.W. (D)	5	5
EASTBOURNE	12 1	12 1	SHEERNESS-ON-SEA	20 9	20 6
EDINBURGH	79 6	79 6	SHEFFIELD	37 3	37 3
EXETER	23 8	23 4	SIDMOUTH	13 2	14 2
EXMOUTH (E)	24 2	24 2	SHOREHAM-BY-SEA	11	11
FOLKESTONE (B)	21 3	21	SEAMOUTH (E)	22 10	22 10
FRESHWATER, I.W. (D)	6 4	6 4	SOUTHAMPTON	5	5
GILLINGHAM (Kent) (A)	18 11	18 8	SWANAGE	13 8	13 8
GLASGOW	80 1	89 1	TAVISTOCK	30 5	30 5
GLASTONBURY (F)	16 10	16 10	TUNBRIDGE WELLS WEST	10 6	10 3
GUILDFORD	7 11	7 7	VENTNOR I.W. (D)	5	5
HASTINGS (C)	14 2	13 11	WALBRIDGE	37	37
HERNE BAY	23 8	23 4	WARMINSTER (B)	23	23 8
HORSHAM	8 2	7 11	WELLS (F)	16 10	16 10
HOVE	7 11	7 7	WESTGATE-ON-SEA	26 6	26 2
ILFRACOMBE	29 8	29 5	WEYMOUTH	16 3	16 3
INVERNESS	105	105	WHITSTABLE & TANKERTON	23 1	22 10
LAUNCESTON	32 7	32	WINCHESTER (via Botley)	5 3	5 3
LEEDS	43 1	43 1	WORTHING CENTRAL	6 4	6 1
LEICESTER	26 6	26 6	YARMOUTH, I.W. (D)	5 9	5 6
LEWES (C)	9 5	9 2	YARMOUTH (GREAT)	34 4	34 5
LINCOLN	36	36	YEOVIL	15 2	15 2
LITTLEHAMPTON	5	5	YORK	45 2	45 2

CHILDREN UNDER 14, HALF-FARE. **FIRST CLASS TICKETS ALSO ISSUED**

➤ FOR FARES TO OTHER PLACES APPLY AT BOOKING OFFICE ◄

A—Via London. B—Via Hastings. C—Via Brighton. D—Via Ryde. E—Via Tipton St. Johns. F—Via Templecombe.

TICKETS OBTAINABLE IN ADVANCE AT STATIONS AND AGENCIES.

The return halves of "Monthly Return" tickets issued between stations on the Southern Railway may, if desired, be used for the return journey from any Southern Railway Station to the original starting point, on payment of the difference (if any) in the appropriate fares.

The fares do not include cost of conveyance across London or any other place where the rail journey is not continuous.

LUGGAGE.—Each Passenger may take with him, free of charge, by Rail, 100 lbs. of personal luggage in the case of holders of 3rd class tickets, and 150 lbs. in respect of 1st class tickets.

DOGS, BICYCLES and PERAMBULATORS.—Reduced Rates for return journey by Rail. FOLDED MAIL CARTS conveyed free by Rail.

Waterloo Station, S.E.1.
January, 1939.

GILBERT S. SZLUMPER,
General Manager

Printed in Great Britain.
Waterlow & Sons Limited, London and Dunstable.

C.X. 134/

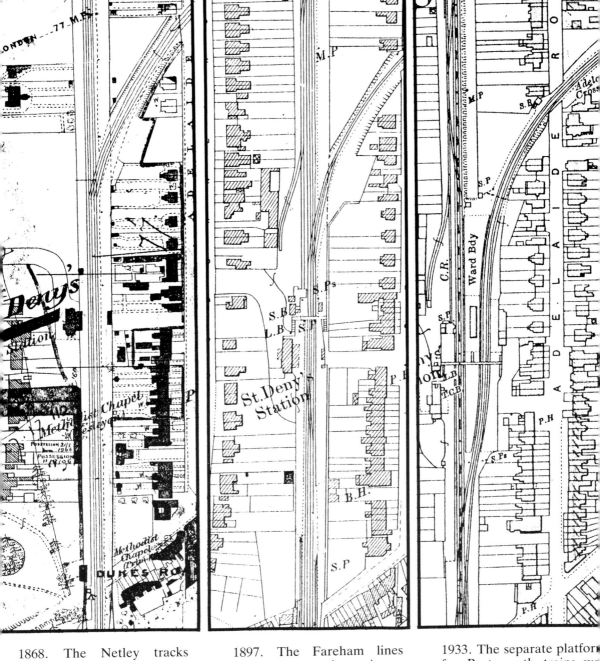

1868. The Netley tracks diverge to the right and merge to single line just to the east of Adelaide Road. Until 1876 it was called Portswood – this map shows a later amendment.

1897. The Fareham lines merge closer to the station; a signal box stands on the up platform and the goods yard has two sidings.

1933. The separate platform for Portsmouth trains were provided in 1899 and the line southward were quadrupled in 1902.

82. The first station in the area was Portswood and was opened on 1st May 1861. It was further north, close to St. Denys Road, until the junction was made. Here we witness a Portsmouth to Southampton train leaving the 1899 platforms, hauled by Adams class 460 no. 464. (Lens of Sutton)

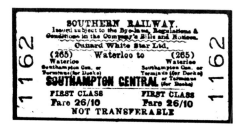

83. The two sidings of the goods yard are just visible but more obvious are the additional curves put into the branch lines when the separate platforms were provided. East-bound drivers often had unkind thoughts about it as they attempted to restart up the 1 in 55 gradient. (Lens of Sutton)

84. GWR trains regularly ran over Southern metals in the Southampton area but this picture was taken nine years after the GWR ceased to exist. Speed record breaking *City of Truro* had been restored for use on special trains but had to earn its daily keep on light trains such as the 2pm Didcot to Southampton Terminus. (S.C. Nash)

85. The impressive gantry replaced two separate posts around 1960. The pairs of signals controlled the two down main lines and the single arms gave access to Bevois Park sidings. N class no. 31816 winds its lengthy van train over the crossing on 18th May 1963, en route for Fratton. (E. Wilmshurst)

All 1.2.3 class.] SOUTHAMPTON and NETLEY.—L. & S.W. [No Sunday Trains.						
Southamptondp	7 30	9 5	10 25	1 45	3 45	5 45	8 0
Portswood	7 36	9 11	10 31	1 51	3 51	5 51	8 6
Bitterne Road	7 39	9 14	10 34	1 54	3 54	5 54	8 9
Woolston	7 45	9 20	10 40	2 0	0 0	0 0	8 15
Sholing	7 49	9 24	10 44	2 4	4 4	4 8	8 19
Netley arr	7 53	9 28	10 48	2 8	4 8	6 8	8 23

Netley dep	8 10	9 35	11 0	2 25	4 30	6 25	8 30
Sholing	8 14	9 39	11 4	2 29	4 24	6 29	8 34
Woolston	8 17	9 42	11 7	2 32	4 37	6 32	8 37
Bitterne Road	8 22	9 48	11 13	2 38	4 43	6 38	8 43
Portswood 38	32	8 27	9 52	11 17	2 42	4 47	6 42	8 47
Southamptn 34	8 35	10 0	11 25	2 50	4 55	6 50	8 55

Bradshaw 1869

86. The east elevation makes an interesting comparison with Woolston and Netley, if you ignore the badly patched wall of the Gents. An unusual feature is that the canopy does not reach the platform edge – more obvious in the picture after next. (D. Cullum)

88. A Cardiff train winds its way past two 20mph restriction signs on 18th April 1981, whilst a new colour light signal stands ready for use under the old gantry. The latter became redundant six months later. (J. Scrace)

---

87. The west aspect still retained its canopy in 1981 and access to the upper floor was by means of an external staircase, seen on the right. Northam gas holder is in the distance. (J. Scrace)

LONDON & SOUTH WESTERN
RAILWAY.   787
TO
Portswood

89. The signal box was more impressive from the front, where there were eight windows. It ceased to function on 11th October 1981, when mechanical signalling ended. To the south, there were once over 24 sidings which were reduced by 1976 to a few serving a Schweppes depot, M.A.T. Cartrain and Baker's. (J. Scrace)

90. South of Bevois Park sidings, Mount Pleasant Crossing spans four tracks. The gates were replaced by barriers prior to the closure of the box on the same day as St. Denys. (J. Scrace)

91. Looking south from Mount Pleasant crossing in 1970, we see the two reception roads and some of the twelve sidings of Northam Yard or Mulfords sidings. The array of up signals are worth a closer look. At the north end of the yard, near the cement silos, a line curved east to reach the Itchen Wharves and, until 1903, there was a 14-road locomotive shed on the site. (D. Cullum)

92. Northam Junction was at the apex of the triangular junction. At this point the quadruple track ends and the branch to Dibles Wharf begins. (This name has been frequently mis-spelt Dibbles). The signal box closed at the same time as its two northern neighbours. The DEMU is bound for Salisbury on 18th July 1974. (J. Scrace)

93. Class B4 no. 30096 worked for most of its life in Southampton Docks and was purchased in 1963 by P.D. Fuels Ltd to work at Dibles Wharf. It is seen there in 1971 and in 1972 it was moved to the Bluebell Railway for preservation. In earlier years locomotive coal had been unloaded there from ships but in 1966 a coal concentration depot was established. In 1986, several four-wheeled hopper wagons arrive daily and are taken across two streets by the firm's 0–6–0 Hunslet, under the protection of the traditional red flag. (J. Scrace)

The 1931 map of 6″ scale gives an impression of the extent of the railways of the area. South of the gas works complex, the Chapel Tramway branches off to serve numerous quays. The black circles indicate gas holders.

94. Residential and commercial development of the area was commencing when the station opened on 1st December 1872. Looking north, in about 1900, we see the previous Northam Junction box which lasted until 8th July 1923. (SUIAG)

95. Before the advent of the city's electric tramways, the shelter on the right would have been used by local residents travelling to work at the docks. Access to the booking office was direct from Northam Road. (Lens of Sutton)

96. At about the time of the quadrupling northwards, the bridges were rebuilt and new station facilities were built across the track. By 1923 new additional lines passed behind the station, on the right, for goods traffic to the docks. (D. Cullum collection)

97. This station and the Terminus closed to passengers on 5th September 1966, a few months after this photograph was taken from the footbridge shown in the next picture. The coaches of a London-bound train are in the left background, running on the third side of the triangular junction. The line to Southampton Central (left foreground) ceased to be used in 1973. (D. Cullum)

98. Bevois Street had lost its level crossing in 1964 and in 1966 apparently had dwellings "in need of modernisation", to use house agent's phraseology. The box was made redundant on 2nd October 1966 and for the following seven years the junction was operated from Chapel Crossing box.
(D. Cullum)

99. Chapel Crossing gates were replaced with flashing lights in October 1981 and the box was then closed. By then only a single line remained and was little used.
(D. Cullum)

100. Looking north in 1966, the Chapel Crossing gates are visible on the right and on the left is the site of the former locomotive servicing facilities. The 70ft turntable remains and to the left of the engine stands the yard store and offices. The sign on the roof reads – QUIET PLEASE – SCHOOL. (D. Cullum)

101. Now looking south from the same footbridge we gain our first glimpse of the Terminus, beyond the Central Bridge. On the right is the massive hotel erected by the LSWR for use mainly by their maritime passengers. (D. Cullum)

102. The original terminal building was subject to minor alterations over the years. By 1950, the centre three arches were devoid of doors and the outer two had been filled in with windows, the left hand one forming the frontage of the refreshment room. In 1986, the building was converted into a restaurant and disco. (Lens of Sutton)

103. Platform 1 had a curious reverse curve until alterations were carried out in 1928, after which the six platforms were renum- bered in reverse order. On the right is an open-fronted ground frame. (Lens of Sutton)

104. This June 1939 view shows the dock lines crossing Canute Road in the foreground and the platform canopies in the background. (F.E. Box/NRM)

SALISBURY ANDOVER, SOUTHAMPTON, FAREHAM, GOSPORT, and PORTSMOUTH

Week Days

Miles from Salisbury	Miles	Station	mrn	mrn	mrn	mrn	mrn	mrn	mrn	mrn (From Alton (dep. 7 35 mrn), see page 183)	mrn	mrn	mrn	mrn	mrn	mrn (From Alton (dep. 9 6 mrn) see page 183)
		173 Plymouth (N.R.) ... dep.														
		173 Ilfracombe ... "														
		173 Exeter (Cen.) ... "														
—		Salisbury ... dep.											7 52			
9		Dean											8 9			
12¼		Dunbridge											8 17			
—	Mls	Andover Junction. dep.									6 52					
—	¾	Andover Town									6 56					
—	2¾	Clatford									7 0					
—	5¼	Fullerton									7 6					
—	8½	Stockbridge									7 13					
—	11¾	Horsebridge									7 20					
—	14¼	Mottisfont									7 25					
16¾		Romsey						6 50			7 32	8 0	8 24		8 32	
21¼	—	Chandlers Ford						6 59				8 9			8 41	
23¼	—	Eastleigh A ... arr						7 5				8 15			8 47	
—	20¼	Nursling									7 39		8 30			
—	22	Redbridge									7 43		8 35			
—	23¾	Millbrook									7 48		8 39			
—	24¾	Southampton Central B arr.									7 52		8 43			
		Southampton Central B dep.									7 53		8 44			
—	26¼	Southampton Ter. (for Docks) arr.									7 58					
		Southampton Ter. (for Docks) dep.		5 20			6 35		7 38		8 2					
—	27	Northam					6 38		7 41		8 5					
—	26½	St. Denys		5L36			6U49		7 46		8 9		8 51			
—	27½	Bitterne		5 39			6 52		7 49		8 13					
—	29	Woolston		5 44			6 59		7 55		8 17		8 57			
—	29½	Sholing					7 2		7 58		8 20					
—	31½	Netley		5 50			7 7		8 3		8 25		9 3	9 7		
—	33¼	Bursledon		5 55			7 12		8 8		8 29			9 11		
—	35½	Swanwick		6 0			7 18		8 14		8 35			9 16		
—	—	Eastleigh A ... dep.	1 44		6 45	7 2		7 52							9 3	
29¼	—	Botley			6 55	7 13		8 2							9 13	
32½	—	Knowle Platform								8 31						9 53
35¼	39½	Fareham ... arr.	2 3	6 7	7 6	7 23	7 25	8 13	8 22	8 36	8 42		9 15	9 22	9 23	9 58
—	—	Fareham ... dep.					7 27	8 15							9 30	
38¾	—	Fort Brockhurst					7 34	8 24							9 37	
40¼	—	Gosport ... arr.					7 38	8 29							9 41	
—	—	Fareham ... dep.	2 7	6 8			7 27		8 23		8 43		9 16		9 25	
38¼	42½	Portchester		6 14			7 34		8 29		8 48				9 30	
41	45	Cosham		6 20			7 40		8 35		8 54		9 25		9 36	
—	—	Hilsea Halt		6 25			7 45		8 40						9 40	
44¾	48¾	Fratton		6 29			7 49		8 44		9 2		9 33		9 44	
45½	49½	Portsmouth & Southsea arr.	2 28	6 35			7 53		8 48		9 7		9 37		9 49	
46¼	50¼	Portsmouth Harbour .. "														
88¾	92¾	249 Brighton ... arr.	7 36	8 26			9 36				10a37				1136	

Station	mrn (To Eastleigh arr 9 39 mrn)	mrn	mrn	mrn (Through Train from Reading (G.W.) (dep. 9 10 mrn) see pages 50 and 154)	mrn	mrn (Through Train from Bristol (dep 8 12 mrn))	mrn	aft	aft SX (Saturdays excepted. Arr. St. Denys 12 46 aft.)	aft SO (Saturdays only. Arr. St. Denys 1 2 aft.)	aft (Through Train from Reading (G.W.) (dep 1 10 aft), see pages 50 and 155)	aft (From Alton, (dep. 1 26 aft.) see page 183)	aft	mrn (Through Train Bristol dep. 10 45 mrn. to Southampton Terminus (arr 2 23 aft) see page 188)
173 Plymouth (N.R.) ... dep.														8 28
173 Ilfracombe ... "														8 15
173 Exeter (Cen.) ... "						7 30								1030
Salisbury ... dep.						1029								1 6
Dean						1047								1 22
Dunbridge						1054								1 29
Andover Junction. dep.			9 20				1127							
Andover Town			9 23				1130							
Clatford			9 27				1134							
Fullerton			9 33				1140							
Stockbridge			9 39				1146							
Horsebridge			9 45				1152							
Mottisfont			9 51				1158							
Romsey	8 54	9 22	9 58		1020	11 3	12 5						1 30	1 36
Chandlers Ford		9 31			1029		1214							1 47
Eastleigh A ... arr		9 37			1035		1220							1 55
Nursling		Stop				11 9							1 36	
Redbridge	9 4					1114							1 40	
Millbrook	9 9					1119							1 45	
Southampton Central B arr.	9 12					1123							1 49	
Southampton Central B dep.	9 21					1140							1 51	
Southampton Ter. (for Docks) arr.		mrn												
Southampton Ter. (for Docks) dep.		9 25							1239	1255				
Northam		9 28							1242	1258				
St. Denys	9 28	9 32				1147			1255	1 11			1 58	
Bitterne		9 35				1151			1258	1 15			2 2	
Woolston		9 39				1156			1 4	1 22			2 6	
Sholing		9 42				1159			1 8	1 25			[illegible]	
Netley		9 47				12 4			1 13	1 30			2 14	
Bursledon		9 51				12 9			1 17	1 35			2 18	
Swanwick		9 57				1215			1 23	1 41			2 23	
Eastleigh A ... dep.				1040				1 2			1 44			
Botley				1050				1 12			1 54			
Knowle Platform				10TH56				1THO17				2 14		
Fareham ... arr.		10 4		11 1		1223		1 22	1 30	1 49	2 5	2 20	2 30	
Fareham ... dep.		1016												
Fort Brockhurst		1023												
Gosport ... arr.		1027												
Fareham ... dep.		10 5		11 3		1225		1SO23	1 31	1 51	2 7			
Portchester		1012				1232			1 37	1 58	2 14			
Cosham		1019		1113		1239		1SO35	1 42	2 5	2 21			
Hilsea Halt		1024												
Fratton		1028		1121		1248		1SO44	1 51	2 15	2 30			
Portsmouth & Southsea arr.		1033		1130		1253		1SO48	1 56	2 19	2 35			
Portsmouth Harbour .. "														
249 Brighton ... arr.		1236		1 36		2 36		3SO36	3 36	4 36	4 36			

A Sta. for Bishopstoke.
a Change at Fratton.
B About 1 mile from the Docks & Pier.
L Arr. 5 26 mrn

S O Saturdays only.
S X Saturdays excepted.
THO Thursdays only.
U Arr. 6 42 mrn.

SALISBURY, ANDOVER, SOUTHAMPTON, FAREHAM, GOSPORT, and PORTSMOUTH

Week Days—*Continued*

Station	aft	aft (Through Train from Cheltenham (dep 10 25 mrn))	aft (Through Train from Cardiff (dep 10 30 mrn))	aft	aft	mrn (Through Carr., Plymouth to Portsmouth and Southsea.)	(Restaurant Car Train Plymouth (Friary) dep. 10 10 mrn. to Brighton.)		aft	aft		aft (From Alton (dep. 4 35 aft.) see page 183)	aft	aft
173 Plymouth (N. R.) ... dep						10 19								
173 Ilfracombe ... "														
173 Exeter (Cen.) ... "						12 30								
Salisbury ... dep			1 36			2 50								
Dean														
Dunbridge			1SO55											
Andover Junction ... dep		1 17												
Andover Town		1 22												
Clatford														
Fullerton		1 29												
Stockbridge		1 35												
Horsebridge		1 41												
Mottisfont		1 46												
Romsey		1 54	2 7	2 13	2 58									
Chandlers Ford				2 22	3 7									
Eastleigh A ... arr				2 28	3 13									
Nursling														
Redbridge														
Millbrook														
Southampton Central B arr		2 9	2 23			3 26								
Southampton Central B dep		2 11	2 27			3 28				4 8				
Southampton Ter. (for Docks) arr		2 19								4 13				
Southampton Ter. (for Docks) dep										4 17				5 16
Northam										4 19				5 19
St. Denys			2 37							4 23				5 30
Bitterne			2 41							4 26				5 33
Woolston			2 47							4 30				5 38
Sholing			2 50							4 33				5 41
Netley			2 56							4 38				5 46
Bursledon			3 1							4 42				5 51
Swanwick			3 7							4 47				5 56
Eastleigh A ... dep	2 40												5 30	
Botley	2 50												5 40	
Knowle Platform												5 23		
Fareham ... arr	3 1		3 16			3 55				4 54		5 29	5 50	6 4
Fareham ... dep			3 33						4 30					6 8
Fort Brockhurst			3 40						4 37					6 15
Gosport ... arr			3 44						4 42					6 19
Fareham ... dep	3SO2		3 18			3 58	4 6			4 55			5 51	6 5
Portchester	3SO8		3 26							5 1				6 12
Cosham	3SO14		3 34				4 18			5 6			6 0	6 19
Hilsea Halt										5 11				
Fratton	3SO23		3 44				4 28			5 15			6 9	6 29
Portsmouth & Southsea arr	3SO27		3 49				4 33			5 23			6 15	6 34
Portsmouth Harbour ... "														
249 Brighton ... arr			5 36			5 22				7 10			7a38	

Station	aft (To Bournemouth Central.)	aft (Through Train from Marlborough (dep 3 50 aft))	mrn	aft	aft	aft	aft	aft (Through Train from Bristol (dep 4 36 aft))	aft (From Alton (dep. 8 0 aft.) see page 183)	aft	aft		aft (Arrives St. Denys at 10 7 aft.)	aft (To Eastleigh, arr 11 1 aft.)	aft (Through Train from Exeter (Central))
173 Plymouth (N. R.) ... dep			1129								1 0				4 49
173 Ilfracombe ... "			1220								3 10				4 45
173 Exeter (Cen.) ... "			2 30								5 53				7 50
Salisbury ... dep			5 5					7 0			8 28			9 55	11 0
Dean			5 22					7 17			8 43			1012	
Dunbridge			5 30					7 26			8 51			1019	
Andover Junction ... dep		4 41					6 46			7 34					
Andover Town		4 46					6 49			7 39					
Clatford		4 51					6 53			7 44					
Fullerton		4 56					6 59			7 50					
Stockbridge		5 3					7 5			7 57					
Horsebridge		5 9					7 12			8 4					
Mottisfont		5 15					7 18			8 10					
Romsey	5 0	5 22	5 38	5 57			7 25	7 34		8 19	8 58			1028	11WSO
Chandlers Ford	5 10			6 6			7 35			8 29	9 8				
Eastleigh A ... arr	5 20			6 12			7 41			8 35	9 20				11 38
Nursling		5 28						7 42							
Redbridge		5 33													
Millbrook		5 38													
Southampton Central B arr		5 42	5 53					7 52						1043	
Southampton Central B dep		5 44	5 55					8 0						1044	
Southampton Ter. (for Docks) arr		5 50													
Southampton Ter. (for Docks) dep					6 15								10 0		
Northam					6 18								10 3		
St. Denys			6 3		6 22			8 9					1013	1051	
Bitterne					6 25			8 13					1016		
Woolston			6 9		6 30			8 19					1021		
Sholing					6 33			8 22							
Netley			6 15		6 38			8 29					1027		
Bursledon			6 19		6 42			8 34					1031		
Swanwick					6 48			8 40					1036		
Eastleigh A ... dep						7 30					9 26				
Botley						7 40					9 38				
Knowle Platform									8 48						
Fareham ... arr			6 29		6 55	7 51		8 48	8 54		9 48		1043		
Fareham ... dep									8 55						
Fort Brockhurst									9 3						
Gosport ... arr									9 7						
Fareham ... dep			6 30		6 56	7 53		8 50			9 52		1044		
Portchester					7 2	8 0		8 57			9 58		1050		
Cosham			6 39		7 7	8 6		9 5			10 5		1055		
Hilsea Halt					7 12										
Fratton			6 48		7 16	8 16		9 16			10 13		11 4		
Portsmouth & Southsea arr			6 53		7 20	8 20		9 19			10 18		11 9		
Portsmouth Harbour ... "															
249 Brighton ... arr			8 36		9 36	10a37									

1942 timetable

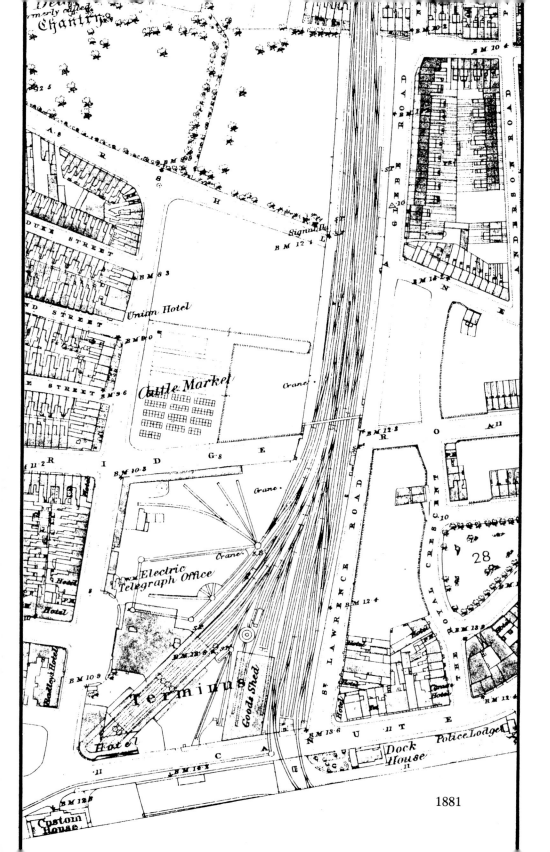

1881

105. Three GWR locomotives at once could give the impression that this was not a SR station. On the left is a Duke class and double heading are a Dean 2301 class and an ex- MSWJR 0–6–0. The tram standards on Central Bridge date the photograph as before 1948. (D. Cullum collection)

106. Standard class 5 4–6–0 no. 73020 departs on 18th September 1965. Services from Cheltenham, Didcot and local trains had regularly terminated here. The area.is now an uninteresting car park. (E. Wilmshurst)

107. On 20th March 1966, a RCTS railtour reversed here. Class 4 no. 75070 is seen awaiting departure time, with the massive goods shed in the background. This was subsequently occupied by NCL and Pickfords. (D. Fereday Glenn)

108. The signal box was curiously not named after the station. Passenger services ceased on 9th September 1966 but the station was reopened for parcels from 11th November 1966 until March 1968. The signal box closed on 13th December 1970. (J. Scrace)

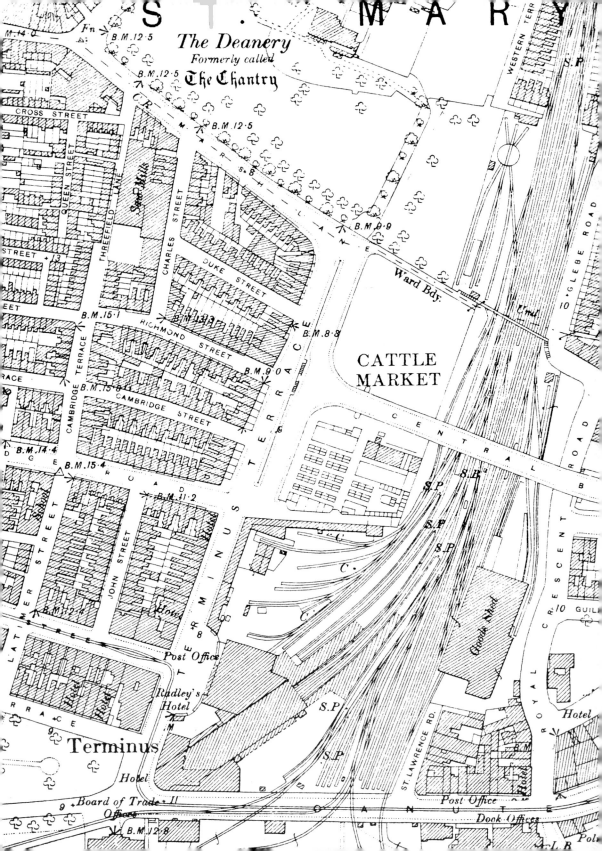

S · T · M A R Y

CROSS STREET

WESTERN TERR.

The Deanery
Formerly called
The Chantry

B.M.12·5

B.M.12·5

B.M.12·5

GLEBE ROAD

B.M.9·9

Ward Bdy.

CATTLE
MARKET

B.M.15·1

B.M.13·3

B.M.8·8

RICHMOND STREET

B.M.9·0

CAMBRIDGE TERRACE

B.M.15·6

CAMBRIDGE STREET

CENTRAL

ROAD

B.M.14·4

B.M.15·4

S.B.

S.P.

B.M.11·2

S.P.

S.P.

JOHN STREET

C.

C.

LATIMER STREET

B.M.12·4

Goods Shed

C.

CRESCENT

ROYAL

10 GUIL

Post Office

Radley's
Hotel

S.P.

ST. LAWRENCE RD.

Hotel

Terminus

S.P.

Hotel

Board of Trade
Offices

Post Office

Dock Offices

B.M.12·8

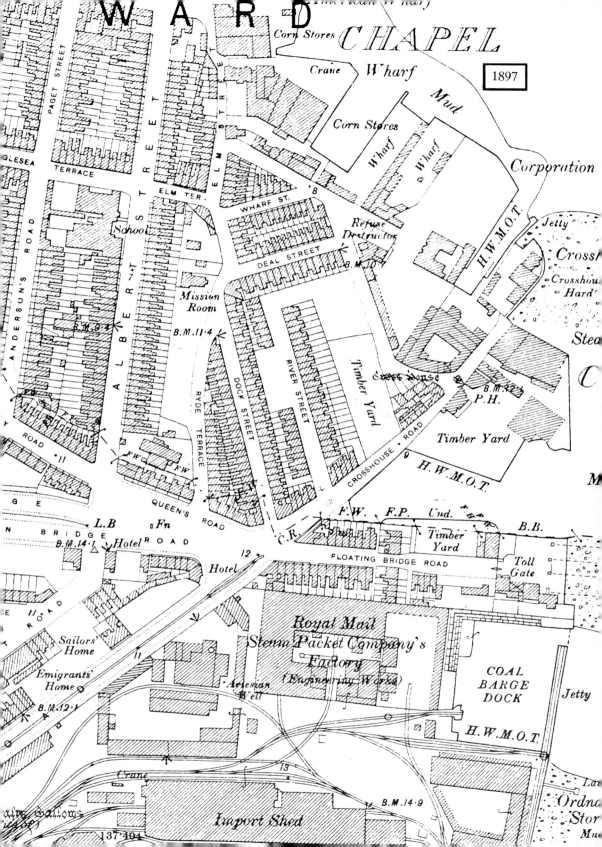

SOUTHAMPTON DOCKS

109. The boundary of the Docks is the wall on the right of this view of Canute Road. This LSWR class B4 0–4–0T no. 91 is hauling cattle wagons into the Docks in about 1908. The white areas on the trucks are due to an antiseptic lime wash. (SUIAG)

110. Class 5 no. 73022 crosses in the opposite direction with a Shaw Saville Boat Train on 29th September 1966. The red flags gave way to red flashing lights in October 1981. (D. Fereday Glenn)

111. This ground frame was opened on 18th December 1955 and was on the north side of Canute Road, adjacent to the station. The previous one had been on the opposite side of the tracks. (J. Scrace)

112. The Royal Pier station opened in January 1891 and was served by short trains which were often hauled by condensing engines. In the following year the LSWR bought the Docks which started a long association between the railway and the shippers. (D. Cullum collection)

113. Initially steamers served Ryde, Portsmouth and Cowes but eventually services were concentrated on the latter town.

114. A view towards the land shows one of the Docks Co's saddle tanks and the severe curvature of the platforms. This postcard was

The carriage doors seem to be open on the wrong side of the train – was Toujours Whisky too well advertised? (Lens of Sutton)

produced not long before services ceased in September 1914. (Lens of Sutton)

115. From left to right – Homeric, Olympic, Berengaria and Aquitania in about 1922 at the Ocean Dock. Their combined bulk tends to distract one from the interesting railway scene in the foreground. (SUIAG)

116. Over 20 class B4s were built between 1891 and 1908, for use in the Docks mainly. No. 90 is seen here in July 1935 displaying its linseed filtrator behind the dome. These devices were used between 1929 and 1938 to reduce impurities in the boiler water. (S.W. Baker)

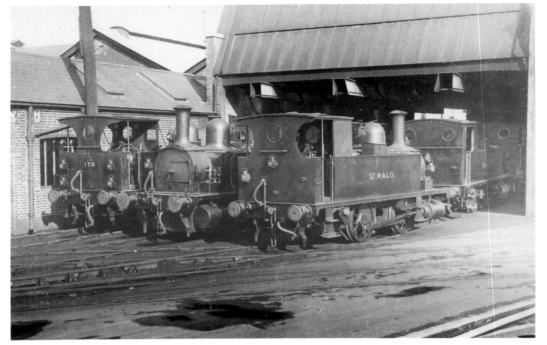

117. The docks shed, with a group of B4s, was photographed on 8th March 1936, on which day there were fourteen B4s and three D1 0–4–2Ts allocated and there were fourteen separate regular duties in the docks. (H.N. James)

118. The Ocean Terminal was opened 31st July 1950 and contained two full length platforms for main line trains. It was supplied with telescopic gangways to link with the ships and marked the high point in transAtlantic travel before the airways removed the traffic. The Queen Mary is seen dressed overall for the Queen's birthday on 4th August 1950. (S.W. Baker)

119. During WWII a large number of 0–6–0Ts were built in the USA for use in Europe. After the war, the SR purchased a number which were mainly used in the Docks. This August 1960 view shows the bows of the Queen Elizabeth and north end of the Ocean Terminal. The latter was last used on 1st December 1980. (H.N. James)

120. In 1929, the SR started the construction of a major new Dock with quays extending for nearly two miles along the River Test. More recently a container terminal has been developed near Redbridge. The old Eastern Docks has declined in importance and this view shows D 206 entering the Docks in May 1962 with a special train from Liverpool. In 1986, the only rail traffic to the Western Docks is an occasional train such as this, for a liner and a small amount of freight, mainly imported motor vehicles. (E. Wilmshurst)

MP *Middleton Press*

Easebourne Lane, Midhurst, West Sussex, GU29 9AZ
☎ Midhurst (073 081) 3169

BRANCH LINES
BRANCH LINES TO MIDHURST	0 906520 01 0
BRANCH LINES TO HORSHAM	0 906520 02 9
BRANCH LINE TO SELSEY	0 906520 04 5
BRANCH LINES TO EAST GRINSTEAD	0 906520 07 X
BRANCH LINES TO ALTON	0 906520 11 8
BRANCH LINE TO HAYLING	0 906520 12 6
BRANCH LINE TO SOUTHWOLD	0 906520 15 0
BRANCH LINE TO TENTERDEN	0 906520 21 5
BRANCH LINES TO NEWPORT	0 906520 26 6

SOUTH COAST RAILWAYS
BRIGHTON TO WORTHING	0 906520 03 7
WORTHING TO CHICHESTER	0 906520 06 1
CHICHESTER TO PORTSMOUTH	0 906520 14 2
BRIGHTON TO EASTBOURNE	0 906520 16 9
RYDE TO VENTNOR	0 906520 19 3
EASTBOURNE TO HASTINGS	0 906520 27 4
PORTSMOUTH TO SOUTHAMPTON	0 906520 31 2

SOUTHERN MAIN LINES
WOKING TO PORTSMOUTH	0 906520 25 8
HAYWARDS HEATH TO SEAFORD	0 906520 28 2
EPSOM TO HORSHAM	0 906520 30 4

STEAMING THROUGH
STEAMING THROUGH KENT	0 906520 13 4
STEAMING THROUGH EAST HANTS	0 906520 18 5
STEAMING THROUGH EAST SUSSEX	0 906520 22 3

OTHER RAILWAY BOOKS
INDUSTRIAL RAILWAYS OF THE SOUTH-EAST	0 906520 09 6
WAR ON THE LINE The official history of the SR in World War II	0 906520 10 X
GARRAWAY FATHER AND SON The story of two careers in steam	0 906520 20 7

OTHER BOOKS
MIDHURST TOWN – THEN & NOW	0 906520 05 3
EAST GRINSTEAD – THEN & NOW	0 906520 17 7
THE GREEN ROOF OF SUSSEX A refreshing amble along the South Downs Way	0 906520 08 8
THE MILITARY DEFENCE OF WEST SUSSEX	0 906520 23 1
WEST SUSSEX WATERWAYS	0 906520 24 X
BATTLE OVER PORTSMOUTH A City at war in 1940	0 906520 29 0